COOL CARS

McLAREN 750S

BY KAITLYN DULING

EPIC

BELLWETHER MEDIA ››› MINNEAPOLIS, MN

EPIC BOOKS are no ordinary books. They burst with intense action, high-speed heroics, and shadows of the unknown. Are you ready for an Epic adventure?

This edition first published in 2025 by Bellwether Media, Inc.

No part of this publication may be reproduced in whole or in part without written permission of the publisher. For information regarding permission, write to Bellwether Media, Inc., Attention: Permissions Department, 6012 Blue Circle Drive, Minnetonka, MN 55343.

Library of Congress Cataloging-in-Publication Data

LC record for McLaren 750S available at: https://lccn.loc.gov/2024002292

Text copyright © 2025 by Bellwether Media, Inc. EPIC and associated logos are trademarks and/or registered trademarks of Bellwether Media, Inc. Bellwether Media is a division of Chrysalis Education Group.

Editor: Rachael Barnes   Designer: Jeffrey Kollock

Printed in the United States of America, North Mankato, MN.

TABLE OF CONTENTS

A CITY DRIVE	**4**
ALL ABOUT THE 750S	**6**
PARTS OF THE 750S	**12**
THE 750S'S FUTURE	**20**
GLOSSARY	**22**
TO LEARN MORE	**23**
INDEX	**24**

A CITY DRIVE »

The stoplight turns green. The McLaren 750S tears down the street!

This **supercar** rides low. But the driver presses a button. The car's nose lifts in four seconds! The 750S rolls smoothly over bumps in the road.

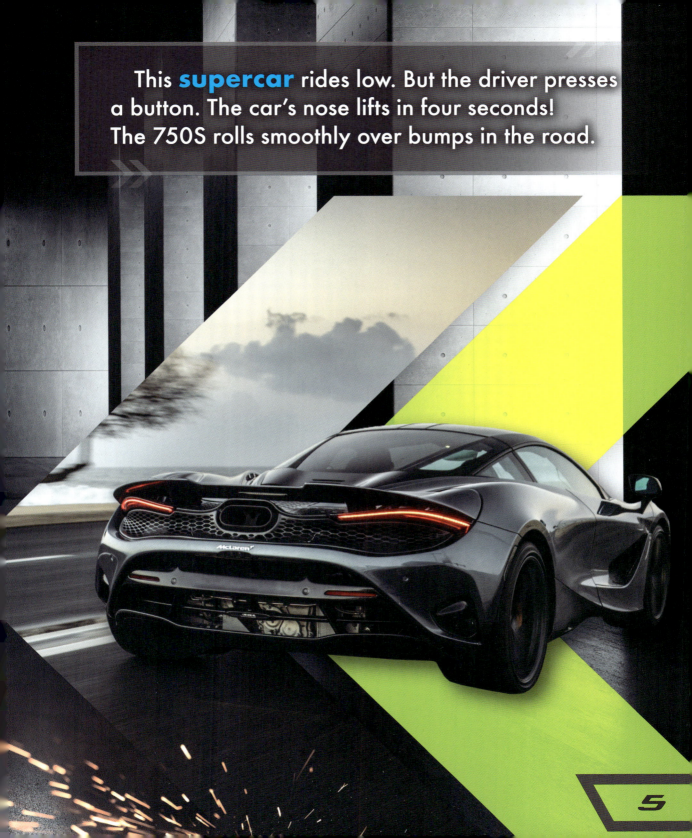

ALL ABOUT THE 750S »

BRUCE MCLAREN RACING IN 1963

McLaren started as a New Zealand racing team. It was formed by Bruce McLaren in 1963. Later, the company made road cars.

Today, McLaren builds fast and flashy cars in England. The P1 and the Senna are famous **models**.

SENNA

📍 WHERE IS IT MADE?

WOKING, ENGLAND

EUROPE

7

The 720S was sold from 2017 to 2023. Fans loved it! The 750S replaced it in 2023. The 750S is more powerful. It picks up speed faster. Some say it is more fun to drive!

LIGHT AND SPEEDY

The 750S is more than 65 pounds (29.5 kilograms) lighter than the 720S. That helps make it fast!

720S

750S BASICS

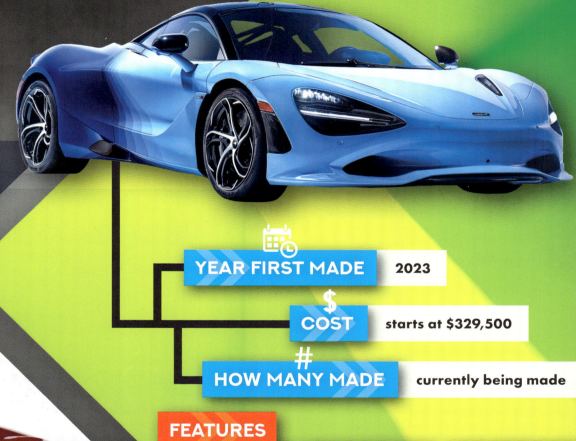

YEAR FIRST MADE — 2023

COST — starts at $329,500

HOW MANY MADE — currently being made

FEATURES

frunk

air intakes

McLaren Control Launcher

Some McLaren models are track-only. But the 750S is built for daily driving.

SPORTY STORAGE

Instead of a trunk, the 750S has a front trunk. It is called a frunk!

This supercar can drive up to 206 miles (332 kilometers) per hour!

PARTS OF THE 750S »

The 750S has a powerful **V8 engine** with a thundering growl. As the car speeds up, it gets louder and louder!

Buyers can add a window to see the engine from inside the car.

🛠️ ENGINE SPECS

TWIN-TURBO V8 ENGINE

TOP SPEED	206 miles (332 kilometers) per hour
0-60 TIME	2.7 seconds
HORSEPOWER	740 hp

The 750S has hidden **air intakes**. They move air through the car to cool the engine.

AIR INTAKE

SIZE CHART

WIDTH 85.1 inches (216.1 centimeters)

Special doors on the 750S open upwards. Part of the roof stays attached!

16

750S SPIDER

The 750S Spider is a **convertible**. Its roof can be lowered in just 11 seconds.

17

Drivers can choose from three drive modes. Comfort mode is for daily driving. Track mode is for racing. Sport mode is extra loud and fast!

Inside, the 750S is simple. It can be dark or brightly colored.

READY TO LAUNCH

The McLaren Control Launcher (MCL) was first included in the 750S. Drivers press the MCL button to store car settings between trips.

MCL BUTTON

THE 750S'S FUTURE »

The 750S will be McLaren's last fully gas-powered car. Instead, McLaren is starting to make **hybrid** supercars. Some parts are **3D-printed**!

In the future, McLaren plans to build its first **SUV**. This four-door car will be **electric**!

McLAREN HYBRID CAR

GLOSSARY

3D-printed—created with a 3D printer; 3D printers make layers of material using directions from a computer.

air intakes—openings on a car that allow air to reach its engine

convertible—a car with a folding or soft roof

electric—able to run without gasoline

hybrid—related to a car that uses both a gasoline engine and an electric motor for power.

models—specific kinds of cars

supercar—an expensive and high-performing sports car

SUV—a car that often sits higher off the ground and can drive off-road; SUV stands for sport utility vehicle.

V8 engine—an engine made with 8 cylinders arranged in the shape of a "V"

wing—a part on a car's body that helps it smoothly travel through the air; some wings can also move to help cars stop quickly.

TO LEARN MORE

AT THE LIBRARY

Adamson, Thomas K. *McLaren 720S*. Minneapolis, Minn.: Bellwether Media, 2023.

Colson, Rob. *Supercars*. New York, N.Y.: Crabtree Publishing, 2022.

Duling, Kaitlyn. *McLaren Elva*. Minneapolis, Minn.: Bellwether Media, 2024.

ON THE WEB

Factsurfer.com gives you a safe, fun way to find more information.

1. Go to www.factsurfer.com.

2. Enter "McLaren 750S" into the search box and click 🔍.

3. Select your book cover to see a list of related content.

INDEX

3D-printed, 20
air intakes, 14
basics, 9
colors, 19
company, 6, 7, 10, 20, 21
convertible, 17
doors, 16, 20
drive modes, 18
electric, 20
engine, 12, 13, 14
engine specs, 12
frunk, 11
future, 20
gas-powered, 20
history, 6, 8, 19
hybrid, 20, 21
inside, 19
McLaren, Bruce, 6
McLaren Control Launcher, 19

models, 7, 8, 10, 17
New Zealand, 6
nose, 5
roof, 16, 17
size, 14–15
speed, 7, 8, 11, 12, 18
Spider, 17
supercar, 5, 11, 20
SUV, 20
weight, 8
window, 12, 13
wing, 15
Woking, England, 7

The images in this book are reproduced through the courtesy of: McLaren, front cover, 3, 4, 5, 7, 8 (main and 720S), 9 (isolated, intake, frunk, and MCL), 10, 11, 12, 13 (main and window), 14 (main and window), 15 (main and length), 16, 17, 18, 19, 20, 21; Bernard Cahier/ Getty Images, p. 6.